EDUCATE GIRLS
AROUND THE WORLD

Good People Doing Good Work

Shay Spivey, BSW, MSW

Educate Girls Around The World

EDUCATE GIRLS AROUND THE WORLD
GOOD PEOPLE DOING GOOD WORK

EDUCATE GIRLS AROUND THE WORLD
GOOD PEOPLE DOING GOOD WORK
2017

By
Shay Spivey, BSW, MSW

Foreword by Dr. Judith Gill

This book is for educational purposes. Every effort has been made to ensure that the information contained in this book is accurate at the time of publication and all relevant sources have been cited.

Interpretations or conclusions should be understood to be solely those of the author or those of the cited reference.

Cover by McLabz Solutions

Edited by Finesse Writing and Editing LLC

Design by Shay Spivey

DEDICATION

To every girl and woman on this earth,

especially my daughters,

You are worthy.

You are worth it.

Your life means something.

I am fighting for you!

Educate Girls Around The World

TABLE OF CONTENTS

ACKNOWLEDGEMENTS

Educate Girls Around the World would not have been possible without the collaboration and contributions of many people and organizations.

THANK YOU to ALL the organizations that educate girls around the world. Your work to meet the global challenge of girl's education is appreciated.

THANK YOU for each new graduate!
THANK YOU for every new school you build!
THANK YOU for every new area that you expand into! Keep fighting the good fight!

THANK YOU to the Half the Sky Movement, which changed the trajectory of my life. It awakened my passion and desire to learn more about the lives of women everywhere. THANK YOU to Oprah Winfrey for being courageous and for sharing your vision for girls' education – I was listening!

I would like to extend a special THANK YOU to Dr. Judith Gill for the beautifully written foreword. I appreciate Dr. Gill lending her expertise, 30 years of experience in education, and extensive research into gender and its associations with achievement and working lives. It was an honor to work with you.

THANK YOU to each organization and individual that contributed to the creation of this book. I appreciate all your support as well as every piece of material, shared experience, quote, photo, and personal interview. A special THANK YOU to Emily Hoppes, Joy Lynn Alegarbes, Valentine Samoei, Dr. Carolyn Gentle-Genitty, LaShaila Spivey, Felicia Ernest, Raichle Farrelly, and Verona Robinson, and everyone that responded to the call!

Last but never least; I want to thank my family and friends for all your love and support – Maya and Tylin.

FOREWORD

After having spent many years working in teacher's education, specifically to develop students understanding of gender and the ways it can impact young lives, I was delighted to be contacted by Shay Spivey and to hear her lively and energetic plan to contribute to the promotion of girls' education from a global perspective. I think this approach has great value as it involves a re-analysis of what is happening to girls in our current schooling as well as highlighting the connections between gender and culture in other places. For some time, teacher education has moved from a general concern about girls' education to a current focus on boys as being the most needy in terms of educational outcomes. And yet I do not share the widely held opinion that girls' issues have been 'fixed' and that 'it's all equal now.' In my recent book *A Girl's Education: Schooling and the Formation of Gender, Identities and Future Visions,* I've tried to set out the reasons for my concern.

Educate Girls Around The World

The sense of a crisis in girls' education is immediately evident from the statistics in the developing world. A quick glance at development studies reveals enormous differences in the likely fates of girls and boys in many third world countries. For example, in 2012 in Northern Ghana 65 percent of girls over age 15 were found to have received no formal education, as a result of living in extreme poverty in a culture whose limited resources determine that males are more likely to benefit from education than females (Camfed Ghana, 2012). In India, girl children are more likely to be abandoned by parents in their desperate need to maximize their son's potential for assisting them to survive into old age (Times of India, 2011). In Pakistan in 2006, 60 percent of children not in school were girls, in Cambodia's hill provinces girls were five times more likely than boys to be absent from school and in Nigeria only 12 percent of poor Hausa girls went to school (Unterhalter & North, 2011). Of the world's 130 million out-of-school youth, 70 percent are girls (Mitchell and Reid-Walsh, 2012).

At times, stories from the developing world function to alert the west to important principles. For example, the abduction of 200+ schoolgirls in Nigeria provoked global outrage. Some reports describe Boko Haram as an Islamic extremist group who regard western education as sinful, most especially in terms of girls whose main sociocultural obligation is to stay at home and have babies. The shocking incident provoked international outrage and is yet to be resolved. Once again it is an example of the interaction between gender, local culture, education, and power.

Widespread recognition of the need for action on girls' education in the developing world has been taken up across many parts of the developed world. In 2015, Michelle Obama launched the White House's *Let Girls Learn* initiative, writing:

> *Right now, 62 million girls worldwide are not in school. They're receiving no formal education at all—no reading, no writing, no math—none of the basic skills they need to provide for themselves and their families, and contribute fully to their countries.*
>
> (Shapiro, Forbes Magazine, Nov. 7, 2015)

Educate Girls Around The World

Researchers involved with the promotion of education for girls in the developing world have commented that the majority of such projects are frequently grounded in fairly traditional notions of girls and women. Thus, the rationale for educational interventions is presented in terms of women's child rearing and household managing roles rather than the potential for educated women to access public positions and contribute to decision making. Such concerns do not counteract the evident value of developing basic education systems that are gender inclusive.

Not so long ago across the English speaking world, girls' education operated in very different parameters from that of boys. Girls were trained to be wives and mothers while boys were educated for the workforce. Changes in the world of work, coupled with current economic conditions meant that from mid last century more and more girls understood themselves as likely to be in paid work for most of their adult lives, and slowly but surely girls' education changed accordingly. At the same time, there continue to be stark gender differences in educational outcomes and career choices in many areas and the 20 percent gender gap in earning power between men and women continues to apply despite strenuous efforts to overcome it.

For all of these reasons and many more I commend Shay Spivey's project and, given her proven expertise in promoting access to education for disadvantaged groups, I have high hopes that it will be a continuing and deeply rewarding enterprise. Certainly the insertion of her lively approach and considerable energy provide a real encouragement for readers to become involved and ready to tackle this ongoing inequity. For readers, wherever you are, keep in mind the maxim to start local and then grow into global because a global effort is needed for global problems.

Foreword written by
Judith Gill, PhD
Adjunct Associate Professor
University of South Australia
Coauthor of *A Girl's Education, Schooling and the Formation of Gender, Identities and Future Visions*
(2017)

Every girl, no matter where she lives, no matter what her circumstance, has a right to learn.

Malala Yousafzai

#EDUCATEGIRLSAROUNDTHEWORLD

BRIEF SUMMARY

Around the world, **62 million girls are not in school**, and millions more are fighting for the education they deserve. This book was written to help bring awareness to the importance of educating girls and to highlight the organizations that are making a difference in the field of global education - especially for girls.

Good people doing good work.

I hope that you, the reader, will gain a better understanding about the problems and opportunities in girls' education around the world. I hope that you use this knowledge as motivation to **BE THE CHANGE**.

#62Million

INTRODUCTION

Educate Girls Around The World

INTRODUCTION

Over sixty years ago, in the Universal Declaration on Human Rights in 1948, education was declared a fundamental human right for everyone.

Yet, there are 62 million girls worldwide who are not in school, and millions more are fighting for the education they deserve. This book is a celebration of good people doing good work in the global movement for girls' education.

Educate Girls Around the World is a celebration of the progress being made in the global movement for girls' education. This book showcases organizations that are making a difference in the field of global education – especially for girls. I also point out how education positively impacts a number of major issues that girls and women face in the developing world.

Organizations Making a Difference

These organizations are the change makers! They are the people at the forefront of the global movement for girls' education. Though girls are being educated at greater numbers than ever before – there is still work to be done. The organizations highlighted in this book are educating girls, building schools, demolishing barriers, breaking the cycle of poverty, training leaders, and creating positive change.

Research shows that education is one of the primary solutions for a number of major issues faced by girls and women worldwide. Studies show that when a girl is educated, she and her family are healthier. Educated girls also live longer, delay marriage, have fewer children, make more money, and are less likely to tolerate physical and sexual violence or be manipulated into human trafficking. Education is the best antidote for poverty, oppression, and terrorism.

> *We're in this together. Because these girls are our girls. They are us. They each have the spark of something extraordinary inside of them just like our daughters - and our sons - and their fate is very much our responsibility.*

Michelle Obama
Former First Lady of the United States

Educate Girls Around The World

Goals

(1) Let's celebrate the girls' education advocates that are making a difference today:

There are countless organizations making a difference in global education - especially for girls. We may hear about an organization or two, here and there, but by gathering all their information and efforts into one compilation, I hope to show the world that there is hope! The organizations mentioned here are leaders in the global movement for girls' education, and these amazing groups of people deserve our full attention and recognition for the extraordinary work they are doing.

(2) Let's celebrate the progress made:

Through the years, we have made great strides toward closing the gender gap in education. Today, more girls have access to good quality education than ever before, and many are enrolling and staying in school longer because the education standards are improving.

(3) Let's raise awareness:

As an advocate for girls' education around the world, I want to raise awareness about several key issues faced by girls and women worldwide - especially education. In areas of the world like Yemen, Afghanistan, Pakistan, Somalia, Saudi Arabia, Sudan, Turkey, Nepal, Niger, Liberia, Mali, Guinea, and Guatemala, girls and women are fighting for the right to learn. In India, China, and many other parts of the world, girls are killed, aborted and abandoned simply because they are female. The United Nations estimates as many as 200 million girls are missing in the world today because of this so-called "gendercide" (It's a Girl, 2012). Women in developing countries are being discriminated to death, and we can no longer turn a blind eye. They face higher mortality rates than their counterparts on the other side of the globe. High rates of illiteracy, poverty, and discrimination are killing women worldwide. Education is the key to addressing all these issues.

(4) Let's inspire and motivate change:
I want to motivate people to get involved. I am inspired by these organizations and fully support the movement for girls' education.

Educate Girls Around The World

Girls' Education Matters

If we don't speak up, who will? It is alarming that more than 62 million girls are not in school. Until every child has access to a good education – we cannot rest. Until the world is a safe place for girls - we cannot rest. Until girls have an equal place in the classroom - we cannot rest. It is our responsibility to ring the alarm – girls' education matters!

Ultimately, I hope that you gain a better understanding about the problems and opportunities in girls' education around the world and use that knowledge to make a difference wherever you are. Girls everywhere need advocates in all areas of education and social justice who are united in a vision that our communities as a whole can become fundamentally stronger and more united when all individuals, male and female alike, receive an education.

Girls have the right to learn.

THIS BOOK

Why is a book like this necessary in the 21st century? Because access to education is a global crisis affecting girls and women worldwide.

This book provides the following:

- A brief introduction to the global movement for girls' education.
- A brief overview of the major challenges girls and women face worldwide.
- A list of the organizations working to educate girls around the world.
- A variety of ways that people can get involved.

The oppression of women and girls is at the top of the international aid community's agenda. Girls face nearly impossible challenges all around the world - just because they are girls. Though not a cure-all, **education** is commonly seen as a primary solution. The global movement for girls' education is growing, and the organizations in this book are working hard at various levels.

Sadly, many girls are denied educational opportunities as the result of extreme poverty, distance, lack of resources, old traditions, the law, and extremist ideas.

There is an abundance of research, academic studies, policy analyses, and evidence that support the benefits of girls' education. Now, it is time to act. The common goal is to enroll more girls and keep them enrolled through 12th grade.

If you educate a man you educate an individual, but if you educate a woman you educate a nation.

African Proverb

GLOBAL MOVEMENT FOR GIRLS' EDUCATION

GLOBAL MOVEMENT FOR GIRLS' EDUCATION

The global movement for girls' education promotes gender equality in education, the enrollment of more girls in school, and the mobilization of resources to help them finish. The movement has come a long way – but the crisis is far from over. It is alarming that more than 62 million girls are not in school. And until every child has access to a good education, we still have work to do. Lack of access and opportunity to a quality education for girls is a global crisis. Especially for girls in developing countries around the world.

Educating girls is proven to have a positive impact on the health, wealth, and safety of communities and societies. One of the most important investments that any country can make in its own future is educating girls.

Educate Girls Around The World

Women make up at least half the world. They are also the primary point of contact for children in most parts of the world. We believe that a mother who has been educated will add to the ripple effect by ensuring that her children are also educated. We believe that when girls are educated, they are empowered to make choices about the direction of their life - when to marry, when to have children, how many children to have, what type of work to do, how to best ensure the health and wellbeing of their children. Some of the girls in our programs have married right after school, but we know that their time in our program has cultivated in them a sense of pride for being educated and literate. Many of our girls have chosen not to marry right after secondary school and have instead opted to continue into vocational school or the workforce, with intentions of starting family later when they are financially secure.

Raichle Farrelly

Executive Director

Girls' Education International

Educate Girls Around The World

The Goals

Around the world, girls and women suffer oppressive discrimination and are denied the fundamental rights experienced by men and boys. The primary objectives of the global movement for girls' education are to:

1. Educate girls at the same rate as boys
2. Help girls complete the same amount of education as boys
3. Reduce the discrimination barriers that girls face regarding going to school
4. Reduce the effects of the lack of education
5. Improve the conditions of girls and women
6. Empower girls and women with the tools needed to rise out of their circumstances

> *If educating every girl will start a chain reaction to end most global issues affecting women – gendercide, sex slavery, oppression, and intense wartime brutality, etc. – then there is much to be done.*
>
> Ginny Carroll
> Founder, Circle of Sisterhood
> Indianapolis, Indiana

Educate Girls Around The World

The Value of Increased Enrollment

Sadly, girls are not educated at the same rate as boys, and millions of girls are missing from primary and secondary schools, even girls living in households with resources (Girls Learn International). All over the world, from Afghanistan to Liberia, girls and women are fighting for the right to learn.

The number of girls missing from primary and secondary schools, as indicated below, emphasizes the heartbreaking truth that school-aged girls are catastrophically under-enrolled:

- 27.9 million girls in Sub-Saharan Africa are not enrolled in school.
- 24.4 million girls in Asia are not enrolled in school.
- 4.3 million girls in Arab states are not enrolled in school.

According to the 2011 Human Development Report of the United Nations Development Program, approximately twice as many males as females receive a secondary education in Pakistan, and public expenditures on education amount to only 2.7 percent of the country's GDP.

For this reason, it is important to increase the enrollment of girls in school that might not otherwise have the opportunity.

Staying in School

Since girls frequently drop out of school before they finish at a higher rate than boys - especially in developing countries - the global movement for girls' education strives to help girls complete the same amount of education as boys.

According to *The top 10 list you don't want to be on: Dangerous places for girls' education,* in 2014, the following regions represented some of the widest gender gaps in secondary school enrollment. In Chad, 46 girls for every 100 boys are enrolled in secondary school:

Country	# of Girls Enrolled Per 100 Boys
Chad	46
Somalia	46
Central African Republic	51
Afghanistan	55
Democratic Republic of the Congo	59
Niger	67
Pakistan	67
Iraq	75
Nigeria	89
India	94

(Winthrop & McGivney, 2014)

We Must Reduce the Barriers

Girls all over the world are fighting for the right to get an education. Unfortunately, some are dying for that right. According to the *Global Coalition to Protect Education from Attack*, girls who seek to attend school face violence and even death in countries ranging from

Nigeria to Pakistan – and too many face sexual abuse even when they are not in school (2014).

In other areas, instead of attending school, some girls face forced marriage, sex trafficking, and child labor. Families living in poverty are often unable to send their daughters to school because they are not able to afford the school fees, books, or uniforms. Eliminating these barriers would make it easier for girls to finish school. Finally, in many countries the route to school itself is long, hard, and dangerous - therefore preventing children from attending.

Literacy Benefits Everyone

What happens to girls who cannot read or write? Of the 774 million illiterate people in the world, two-thirds are women (UNESCO). Girls that never learn these vital, necessary skills are more vulnerable to poverty, human trafficking, child marriage, poor health, and a host of other horrific outcomes. Without job skills, girls are more dependent on others to take care of them, which leads to higher instances of domestic violence and being treated like property. For example, in Nepal, girls are seen as the property of their fathers or husbands for their entire lives.

Education supports a girl's health seeking behaviors and allows her to be a shining example for other young women in her family and community, empowering her to make choices about the life she wishes to lead: who to marry and when, how many children to have and what career to pursue. An educated woman has the knowledge, skills, and self-confidence necessary to be a more informed parent, worker, and citizen.

Joy Lynn Alegarbes
Director of Community
Huru International

Education Improves Lives

By now, you can see that improving the conditions of girls and women around the world is integral to the global movement for girls' education. There is no greater catalyst for economic growth and empowerment while simultaneously improving physical health and reducing discrimination, violence, human trafficking, and child marriage than education.

Investment in girls' education may well be the highest return investment available in the developing world.

Lawrence Summers

Chief Economist, World Bank

Empowerment

It is imperative to empower girls and women with the tools needed to rise above their circumstances. Education has a positive impact on a girl's earning potential and her ability to raise a healthy family. Education gives girls and women a voice. When educated, they acquire the skills, knowledge, and capability needed to change their communities, their countries, and the world.

I would love the world to know that our work is personal, and with continued support we can grow and continue to have a direct impact on girls living in villages, who aspire to do and see so much more in their lives. They know, as do we, that education is the way that they can leverage themselves and their families out of poverty. They know that with an education, they can make a statement like "I want to be a doctor" and believe it to be possible.

Raichle Farrelly

Executive Director

Girls' Education International

Photo provided by HURU International

Women hold up half the sky.

Chinese Proverb

#GIRLSCOUNT

MAJOR

ISSUES

AFFECTING

GIRLS

AND

WOMEN

MAJOR ISSUES AFFECTING
GIRLS AND WOMEN

Education has been proven to have effects on reducing poverty and violence and improving health outcomes for mothers and children.

www.empowerweb.org

On a global scale, girls and women face distinct challenges. Before we can improve their lives, we must explore these challenges in depth as a means to better their outcome. I have isolated seven major concerns for discussion. They include:

- Health
- Death / Extermination
- Violence
- Human Trafficking
- Child Marriage
- Poverty
- Oppression

Health and Related Concepts

- Better Health
- Better Nutrition
- Risk of Disease
- Infant and Maternal Mortality
- Sexual and Reproductive Health

Better Health

Not only does an education benefit the health of girls and women, but it also has a positive effect on their children. When we know better, we do better. When girls are educated, their families are healthier. For every year girls spend in school, their families and communities are healthier. Research shows that a child born to a literate mother is 50 percent more likely to survive past the age of five (UNESCO).

Better Nutrition

When mothers are educated, their families receive better nutrition. Research shows that if all women had a primary education, 1.7 million children would be saved from stunting due to malnutrition. Better still, if all women had a secondary education, 12 million children would be saved stunted growth from malnutrition (UNESCO).

Risk of Disease

One of the added benefits of education is the correlation between disease and infection. Girls that are educated are less likely to contract diseases, such as HIV, AIDS, or malaria because they become more knowledgeable about how diseases are transmitted, thus, they are more likely to use preventive techniques, such as condoms, mosquito nets, and vaccinations. Educated women understand the benefits of better hygiene, regular doctor's visits, providing a quality diet, and treating illnesses. In the long run, higher levels of education lead to healthier children.

Infant and Maternal Mortality

It is estimated that 800 women die every day from pregnancy-related causes that were preventable (World Health Organization, 2016). We can help reduce that number by offering our girls a better education. For every year girls spend in school, they delay having children - reducing the risk of teen pregnancy while simultaneously increasing the infant survival rate beyond age five by 50 percent. According to the World Health Organization, 5.9 million children under the age of five died in 2015. More than half of these early child deaths are due to conditions that could be prevented or treated with access to simple, affordable interventions, such as vaccinations, improved sanitation, and better nutrition (2016).

Complications during pregnancy and childbirth are the second largest cause of death for 15 to 19-year-old girls globally (WHO, 2014). Girls who give birth before the age of 15 are five times more likely to die in childbirth than women in their 20s (Gyesaw, 2013). Research shows that when girls are educated they are more likely to practice safe sex and delay marriage – resulting in fewer adolescent pregnancies.

While death during childbirth is on the decline in many parts of the world, in others women still succumb in growing numbers. For instance, in Niger one in seven women dies during childbirth and in Afghanistan, a woman dies every thirty minutes while delivering a child. Lack of proper health care and hospital facilities also contribute to high rates of death among pregnant women in Somalia.

Education can help prevent the deaths of millions of girls, women, and children around the world. Research shows that the frequency of infant and maternal mortality goes down when women are better educated about health care for their families. For every 1,000 girls educated, 3 less women will die in childbirth (Girls Learn International). Each extra year of a mother's education reduces the probability of infant mortality by 5-10 percent (Let Girls Learn).

Sexual and Reproductive Health

An estimated 225 million women in developing countries have an unmet need for effective modern contraception, which results in more than 74 million unplanned pregnancies and 36 million abortions every year, according to the United Nations Population Fund Guttmacher Institute (UNFPA). We can help girls attend school longer by addressing sexual and reproductive health concerns:

According to Huru International, health is also a major issue that causes young women to struggle to get an education. Young women do not often get the information they need about sexual and reproductive health. They are taught to be ashamed of their menstrual cycles and do not have the products they need to manage their periods safely and with dignity. Girls do not fully understand the connection between starting menstruation and pregnancy. But the people around them do, and expectations shift. They are suddenly seen as "women" who can be married off and start to have sex. And all the while young women are not given the life skills they need to manage these shifting expectations- they do not have the confidence or skills to say "no" to sex when they do not want it, or to negotiate protection when they do. All of these health risks cause girls to struggle in school and eventually drop out.

Emily Hoppes

Program Director and Partner Liaison

Huru International

Sadly, poverty and lack of resources for feminine hygiene products contribute to adolescent girls missing school or dropping out early. As stated by Joy Lynn Alegarbes, Huru International, during a recent baseline survey of Huru International's beneficiaries in rural Kenya, 100 percent of the girls reported that they had missed school for at least one day due to menstruation related challenges. Seventy-three percent of these girls reported missing three or more days a month, specifically due to lack of access to sanitary protection. Missing three days per month translates to a loss of approximately 27 school days each year, per girl. Considering that there are eight lessons in every school day, this means that each girl is missing approximately 216 lessons per academic year.

My school attendances were varied since when my periods came I used to miss classes. My friends used to wonder why I was not coming to school for a week or three days, but I was unable to explain to them. My self-esteem was low then, I used to tell myself that I would not be able to go to my dream school and I won't be able to reach my goals. I used to feel very sorry for myself. I used to have this one wish that I was never born a girl.

– written by a Huru Kit beneficiary about her initial experience with menstruation, before Huru International interventions.

The United Nations estimates as many as
200 million girls are missing in the world today.

Death and Related Topics

- Gendercide
- Female Infanticide
- Female Feticide / Sex Selective Abortion
- Death Dowry
- Abandonment
- One Child Policy
- Son Preference Culture
- Suicide

The three deadliest words in the world... It's a Girl. In India, China and many other parts of the world, girls are killed, aborted and abandoned simply because they are girls.

It's a Girl (2012)

Documentary Film

www.itsagirlmovie.com

Gendercide

Gendercide is defined as the systematic and methodical extermination of girls; the systematic killing of girls. Girls and women around the world are being discriminated to death. Girls are being killed, aborted, and abandoned because women are valued less than men. The world has a responsibility to save girls from the greatest human rights violation of our time.

Female Infanticide

Female infanticide is the practice of killing newborns because they are girls. In India over 25,000 newborn babies are killed every year as midwives are paid to kill baby girls.

According to UNICEF, India is the worst place to be born a girl. In India, the birth of a baby girl is considered a burden. The reason: girls are seen as a financial drain on families due to the cost of a dowry when the daughters get married. Girls are viewed as financial liabilities, while boys are prized for providing their families with additional resources. In traditional Indian marriages, men marry and bring their wives home to take care of his parents. Women, on the other hand, leave the home with a large portion of their family's material wealth.

In India, families are pressured to limit the number of daughters they raise due to the burden of and high costs of the dowry required to marry them off. Families benefit financially by having a son, but if a family has a daughter, it can expect to pay a hefty price to the husband's family.

Female Feticide / Sex Selective Abortion

Female Feticide, also known as Sex Selective Abortion, is the practice of finding out the sex of an unborn child and aborting it if it is a girl – essentially, the practice of terminating a pregnancy based on the predicted sex of the fetus. Today, India and China eliminate more unborn female children than the number of girls born in America every year (It's a Girl, 2012). In 2011, it was reported that in India five million girls are selectively aborted annually. As a result of sex selective abortions, there is a growing gap between the number of boys versus girls in adulthood, which has impacted the population and growth rates in certain countries.

Death Dowry

A death dowry is a term used to describe the deaths of women who are murdered or driven to suicide by continuous harassment and torture by husbands and in-laws in an effort to extort an increased dowry. More than 5,000 women die each year in India as a result of these death dowries - a heinous and brutal crime that is disturbingly common. Husbands and in-laws beat and burn their wives to death when their families cannot pay more money so that they can marry another woman for material gain. Sadly, the majority of the perpetrators go unpunished.

Abandonment

In China and other areas of the world, babies are often abandoned by families simply because they are female. This has resulted in overcrowded orphanages, and young girls becoming victims of sex trafficking and early marriage. Indentured servitude and premature death are equally common.

One Child Policy

From 1979 to 2015, China implemented the One Child Policy, a birth control policy, also known as a population planning measure that restricted families from having more than one child. While the goal was population control, it had the unintended consequence of creating a severe gender imbalance - 37 million more men than women. This has resulted in high rates of female kidnapping and child marriage. Many Chinese women have suffered fines, forced abortions, and forced sterilizations when they have exceeded the one child limit with an "illegal pregnancy." In what can only be described as barbaric, women have been rounded up by family planning officials and forced to abort a second pregnancy, no matter what stage they were in.

> *I was a girl in a land where rifles are fired in celebration of a son, while daughters are hidden away behind a curtain, their role in life simply to prepare food and give birth to children.*
>
> Malala Yousafzai
> *I Am Malala: The Girl Who Stood Up for Education and Was Shot by the Taliban* (2013)

Son Preference Culture

The China One Child Policy and other similar policies have resulted in a son preference culture in several countries. This means that in certain areas of the world, like China and India, boys are perceived as more valuable than girls. Son preference cultures have resulted in high rates of female feticide, female infanticide, abandonment, forced abortions, forced sterilizations, and illegal pregnancies.

Suicide

Suicide needs no definition, but for women in Afghanistan it is a far greater problem than in many countries. In Afghanistan, the average woman only lives to be 45 years old, thanks to an exponentially high suicide rate. Seen as a last ditch effort to escape forced marriage, solitude, control, and abuse, Afghan women commit suicide believing it is their only hope.

Violence Against Women and Related Concepts

- Attacks on Education
- Rape Epidemic
- Domestic Violence
- Honor Killings
- Female Genital Mutilation

No woman, girl, or person, period, should be the subject of a violent attack. However, every day we read stories about women and girls around the world that experience physical or sexual violence. Acts of violence against women – simply because of their gender - demand special attention. Far too often women and girls face horrific treatment and even death just for being born female.

And in recent years, the violence against women and girls that are seeking an education has increased. We must work together to eliminate violence against girls and women.

We are working toward a world where all women and girls can live free from violence – a world where girls can go to school without the fear of being kidnapped, a world where domestic violence no longer exists, a world where women's human rights defenders are not killed for raising their voices, a world where women and girls are not systematically raped during times of instability and war.

Global Fund for Women

Attacks on Education

Girls that try to go to school have become the targets of violent attacks around the world. All too often, young women face hostile environments and brutality and must travel dangerous routes simply to get to school. But why? Because extremist groups with backward ideals forbid girls from becoming educated. Schools have been targeted, and girls have been threatened, beaten, and killed simply for attempting to learn. It is sad to think that in certain parts of Pakistan and Nigeria a goat is considered more valuable than a girl. Here are some of the cases that have made the recent headlines:

Educate Girls Around The World

Nigeria, April 2014 - 276 girls were abducted from the Government Girls Secondary School in Chibok, Nigeria, by the jihadist terrorist organization Boko Haram, whose translation means "Western education forbidden." As of today, most of those girls have not been found.

Nigeria, 2013 - Gunmen threatened, attacked, and killed teachers and students in multiple attacks for teaching "western education." In 2013 alone, more than 50 schools were destroyed or burned down.

Myanmar, 2013 - 200 Buddhist nationalists burned down a Muslim school in Meiktila. 32 students and four teachers were killed.

Pakistan, June 2013 - A bomb killed women teachers and students on a bus in Pakistan.

Afghanistan, 2012 - 160 schoolgirls were poisoned in Afghanistan.

Pakistan, October 2012 - Malala Yousafzai, a 15-year-old Pakistani girl, was shot in the head for promoting girls' rights to an education by the Taliban. The Taliban had outlawed girls school and forced more than 100,000 girls to drop out of school under the threat of violence.

And between 2009 and 2012:

- There were more than 1,110 attacks on schools in Afghanistan.
- 140 teachers were killed and 1,086 received death threats in Columbia.
- More than 838 schools were destroyed, 50 students and teachers were killed, and 138 students and teachers were kidnapped in Pakistan.
- There were 720 reported cases of violence against school in Yemen.

Source: Global Coalition to Protect Education from Attack (2014). *Education under attack 2014.* New York, New York: Global Coalition to Protect Education from Attack.

Rape Epidemic

There is a rape epidemic occurring all over the world. The problem is worse in countries that have no laws or policies to protect women, prevent sexual violence, provide access to justice for victims, or effectively punish offenders.

> *Nearly a billion women and girls around the world will experience rape or sexual abuse over the course of their lives - with violent assaults happening daily. If this violence were a disease, governments and the public would treat it with the urgency and funding appropriate to an epidemic.*
>
> Equality Now
> The World's Shame: The Global Rape Epidemic

Whether by a stranger, family member, friend, or husband - rape is rape – a form of violence that robs a person of control over her own body. Education helps girls and women learn about the law and ways to protect themselves.

Domestic Violence

Despite the fact that we live in the 21st century, women and girls are often treated as property and possessions with no rights and no value - which leads to abuse and neglect. For example, 87 percent of women in Afghanistan have experienced domestic violence at some point in their lives. And in Yemen, 40 percent of women report physical abuse in their lifetime.

Education is a key factor in eliminating this crime. For example, in India, women with no formal schooling are less likely to resist violence than women with schooling (Let Girls Learn).

Honor Killings

An "honor killing," also known as "shame killing," occurs when a person is killed by a family member for bringing a perceived shame or dishonor to the family. The reasons can range from dressing inappropriately, refusing an arranged marriage, having sex outside of marriage, or being a victim of rape. "Honor killing" methods include, but are not limited to, stoning, burning, beating, acid attacks, and shooting.

"Honor killings" persist all over the world. Hundreds of thousands of cases have been documented in Europe, the Middle East, South Asia, the United States, South America, and Australia. In Pakistan, honor killings have become more widespread than ever. For example, married women are frequently killed so that their husbands can marry someone else. In Pakistan, if the family does not approve of someone whom the woman wants to marry, she can be killed to protect the "honor" of the family.

In areas of Pakistan, social mingling of girls and boys is taboo, so when a video of five girls participating in a coed singing party hit the internet, the girls were killed for dishonoring the tribe. The murders were not even considered to be a criminal act (Constable, 2016).

Female Genital Mutilation
Female genital mutilation also known as female circumcision is the act of cutting or removing all or some of the genital organs for non-medical reasons. Female genital mutilation, a traditional cultural practice in areas such as Ethiopia and India, has led to the deaths of countless girls and women around the world. This

unnecessary surgical procedure is practiced in 30 countries around the world - in parts of Africa, Asia, Australia, Europe, the Middle East, and North America. For example, in Somalia, 95 percent of girls between the ages of 4 and 11 have been subjected to female genital mutilation - and often without anesthesia. And thousands of girls die every year from uncontrolled bleeding after being held down and forced to endure this vicious procedure.

This is an outdated and useless practice that has no medical value. Old patriarchal belief systems have kept this barbaric tradition in place for many generations. Education and cultural changes from within these societies can end female cutting for the next generation of young girls. For example, in Burkina Faso, educated women are 40 percent less likely to subject their daughters to genital mutilation (Let Girls Learn).

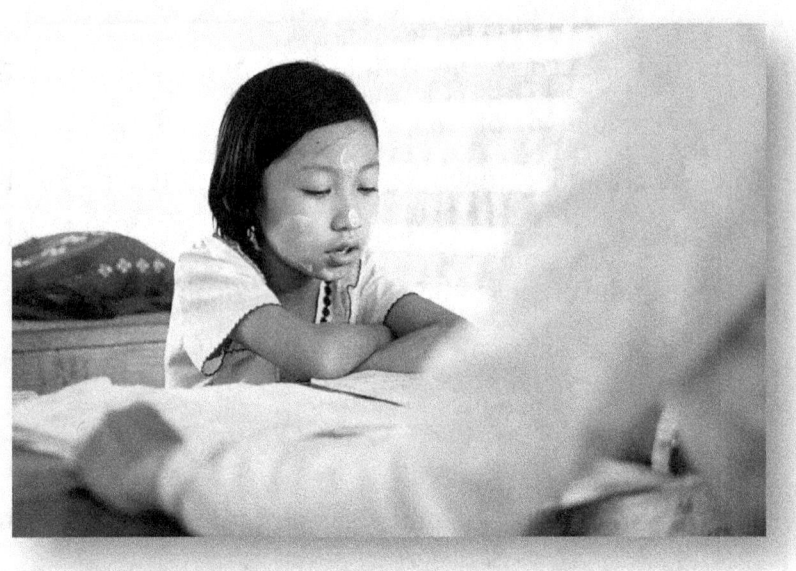

I dream for a world which is free of child labor, a world in which every child goes to school. A world in which every child gets his rights.

Lailash Satyarthi

Indian Child Rights Activist

Founder of Bachpan Bachao Andolan

Nobel Peace Prize Laureate

Human Trafficking and Related Concepts:

- Human Trafficking
- Sex Trafficking
- Child Labor / Forced Labor

Every year hundreds of thousands of men, women, and children are sold into forced labor, prostitution, and child labor, but girls that are educated are less likely to become victims of human trafficking. By increasing girls' education, we can save the lives of millions of girls and women and empower them, thereby giving them a chance at a better life as well as ending the vicious cycle of human enslavement (Polaris, 2017).

> *Education & resources prevent trafficking & provide opportunity.*
>
> The Freedom Project
>
> www.thefreedomproject.org

Human Trafficking

According to the United Nations Office on Drugs and Crime, "human trafficking includes the recruitment, transportation, transfer, and harboring or receipt of persons by means of the threat or use of force or other forms of coercion." Human trafficking is at epidemic levels and, sadly, many young girls are vulnerable to the deceptive tactics of abusers. Since traffickers prey upon the vulnerability of their victims, the less educated are even more at risk of abduction and abuse. Traffickers often promise monetary compensation or other resources in order to achieve the consent of a person having control over another person, even parents themselves, for the purpose of exploitation.

At its core, human trafficking is a form of modern day slavery. The International Labor Organization estimates that there are 20.9 million victims of human trafficking globally.

-68 percent of them are trapped in forced labor;
-26 percent of them are children; and
-55 percent are women and girls.

For example, in India, girls born to poor families, who are not killed at birth, are vulnerable to human trafficking as they are abandoned or sold as child brides and bonded labor.

Sex Trafficking

Let's be clear - there is no such thing as a child prostitute. Children do not choose prostitution. Sex trafficking is a trap and one of the worst forms of child abuse in existence. In Nepal, young girls are often sold to sex traffickers before they reach their teenage years. Traffickers use threats of violence, manipulation, addiction, and debt bondage to keep girls enslaved. Most people know that sex trafficking exists, but they're often shocked to learn that it is taking place right in their own town, city, state, or country. Every night, thousands of girls are being sold for sex in America and abroad. Very few children escape, and many die before they can make it out. Technology, while praised for its innovations, sadly makes it easier to sell children online. For example, traffickers no longer have to parade girls on a street corner; they are able to place free anonymous ads on classified advertisement websites to connect with pedophiles.

India, California, Kenya, Dominican Republic, Georgia, Greece, Indonesia - these would be nice places to visit. Sadly, they're also locations that have active sex trafficking industries. Uneducated

77

and undereducated girls and women are vulnerable to sex traffickers who prey on their weaknesses. Education can be a valuable weapon to fight the war on sex trafficking.

Verona Robinson, BBA

MSHIA Candidate, 2018

Child Labor / Forced Labor

Another form of human trafficking is forced labor or involuntary servitude. This is the largest form of human trafficking across the globe. The International Labor Organization estimates that forced labor and human trafficking is a $150 billion industry worldwide. It is believed that more than 800,000 people are trafficked across international borders each year.

Victims, no matter their age, experience great abuse both physically, emotionally and mentally. They are usually from a vulnerable situation to start with, possibly poor, isolated, child unsupervised, conflict areas, natural disasters or even previously abused.

The Freedom Project

www.thefreedomproject.org

Education is a key strategy in ending human trafficking. First, educating poor children provides the family and children with more options: future earning potential and a way out of poverty. Second, raising awareness brings the multi-billion dollar human trafficking business to light. Educating people about online child pornography, clothing sweat shops, and other forms of human trafficking can help combat the problem by reducing the demand as well as the supply.

Estimates suggest that over 60,000 children are sexually exploited for commercial gain in Thailand each year.

The Freedom Project

www.thefreedomproject.org

#ENDCHILDMARRIAGE

Child Marriage

Culturally, the age at which a person marries is subject to debate, but most people agree that child marriages are fraught with problems. According to Girls Learn International, if nothing changes between now and 2020, there will be 142 million child marriages in developing countries. That's 37,000 girls per day! And girls that marry before the age of 18 are more vulnerable to pregnancy-related death, intimate partner violence, and sexual abuse. For instance, in Nepal, 1 in 24 women die in childbirth or during pregnancy as a result of marriage at an early age.

In South Punjab, where it is legal for a husband to beat his wife, husbands are chosen for Pakistani girls who are sold and traded into early marriages. For instance, in December 2016, it was reported that a Pakistani girl was "traded" for marriage to a 36-year-old disabled man in exchange for a new wife for her father. She was 14, and she had no choice. Also, there are no laws that protect women from being beaten, burned, or killed (Gannon, 2016).

Child marriage is a problem in the developed and developing world:

- 2.9 million girls are married by the age of 15 in Sub-Saharan Africa and South and West Asia, equivalent to one in eight girls in each region (UNESCO, 2014).

- 13.5 million children, most of them girls, will be married before they turn 18 - about 4.4 million of them will be married before they turn 15 (UNFPA, 2015).

- In Afghanistan, more than half of married women are forced into marriage before the age of 16. (*Ten worst countries to be born a woman,* 2016)

In Yemen, one of the poorest and most conservative counties in the Arab world, girls between the ages of 12 and 14 are regularly forced into marriages with adult men. In extreme cases, the girls are sometimes as young as eight years old. Rural areas stricken by poverty have kept up this ancient tradition of child marriage.

Sadly, girls can also be sold to pay their male relatives' debts or lighten a family's financial load. In recent years there have been several reported deaths connected to child marriage – due to internal bleeding on the wedding night.

> *Child marriages are not consensual. They are often arranged because families are unable to financially support the girls, and girls are not considered valued members of society. Education not only increases a girl's self-worth but also increases her earning potential. Education is necessary to erode this selfish and life threatening tradition.*
>
> Verona Robinson, BBA
> MSHIA Candidate, 2018

When girls are educated, they are more likely to delay marriage and are less likely to be forced into one at a young age. Educated girls become empowered women with the skills they need to work, improve their self-esteem, and have more say over their lives. For instance, girls who are educated beyond the 7th grade level tend to marry an average of four years later than their peers (United Nations). And girls with secondary schooling are up to six times less likely to marry as children than those with little or no education (Let Girls Learn).

At the root of it all is the persistence of gender inequality and traditional gender norms. Many parents still believe that their daughters are better off getting married early instead of finishing their education, and communities as a whole undervalue girls' education and girls themselves.

The irony is that undervaluing and hindering girls' education is preventing societies from reaching their full potential. Girls' education is important for a society on every level. When a young woman is educated she is more confident, healthier, and more economically stable. As she gets older, she is able to use her education to improve the lives of her family and her community. Educated girls make future families and communities stronger, which makes for stronger and more successful societies and nations.

Educate Girls Around The World

Emily Hoppes

Program Director and Partner Liaison

Huru International

It's a simple fact. Educating girls is the most powerful and effective way to reduce global poverty.

Mona Foundation

www.monafoundation.org

Poverty

- Decrease the Risk of Extreme Poverty
- Better Employment Opportunities
- Increase Economic Growth

Decrease the Risk of Extreme Poverty

If we want to end poverty, educating girls is one of the primary solutions. According to the International Labor Organization, "educating girls has proven to be one of the most important ways of breaking poverty cycles and is likely to have significant impacts on access to formal jobs in the longer term." (Sperling & Winthrop, 2016).

Educated girls make more money as adults. According to the World Bank, three additional years equates to 30-60 percent more earning power. For example, in Pakistan, working women with a high level of literacy skills earned 95 percent more than women with weak or no literacy skills (Sperling & Winthrop, 2016).

> *Expert studies estimate that every extra year a girl spends in secondary education lifts her income by more than 15 per cent. Better educated girls have better employment and health prospects and,*

as they grow to womanhood, they pass these benefits to their children (Veneman, UNICEF).

Education is an essential tool to help girls acquire the skills and knowledge needed to escape the cycle of poverty by increasing their earning potential and making it possible for them to get better jobs.

Globally, women experience high rates of poverty, and in n the developing world, women often carry the full weight of poverty on their shoulders. As the sole caregivers for children and loved ones, girls are often relegated to domestic duties and child-rearing while boys attend school. As a result, girls are more susceptible to being left behind in poverty and continue to be dependent on their families for support. Conversely, educating both girls and boys would result in greater economic growth for the entire family.

Better Employment Opportunities

Equally as important as the number of years a girl attends school is the quality of that education.

Attending school helps increase individual earnings, but learning well while there and having strong skills to deploy in the labor market help boost earnings even more (Sperling & Winthrop, 2016).

A good quality education provides students with the essential skills and knowledge needed to meet the demands of today's workforce – which in turn increases economic growth for communities. When women have the same skills as men and can create jobs and produce products, the overall economic health is better for everyone.

The world will never realize 100 percent of its goals if 50 percent of its people cannot realize their full potential. When we unleash the power of women, we can secure the future for all.

Ban Ki-moon

UN Secretary General

Increase Economic Growth

Increasing girls' education is the best investment that countries can make for the betterment of their economies. Investment in girls' education should be a priority for governments that want an economic boost. For example, a 1 percent increase in women's secondary education can boost a country's per capita income growth rate by 0.3 percent - which is a generous amount (United Nations).

Research has concluded that if India enrolled 1 percent more girls in secondary school, their GDP would rise by $5.5 billion (Let Girls Learn).

Girls' education is important as any equitable and just society must be able to demonstrate equal opportunities for all its young people to lead fulfilling lives. The recognition of long standing gender–based educational inequity sparked much of the early work on girls' education. In developing countries, girls' education has been identified as a key means of building equity and capacity into local and state communities and as such has attracted a good deal of interest from government aid departments and UNICEF.

Judith Gill, PhD

Educate Girls Around The World

Adjunct A/Professor of Education
University of South Australia

Only when women and girls are safe and free from violence; can earn their own money; can have an equal voice in their family and community; and can decide if, and when, they get married or have children, will we be able to say that they have equality and justice.

Global Fund for Women

Oppression

- Change
- Equality
- Lack of Resources
- Rights
- Empowerment

Change

When girls are educated they become the agents of change in their own household, communities, and society because they gain the self-confidence to speak up and improve situations. For every year a girl spends in school, she gets one step closer to being stronger, independent, and free to choose her future.

Education is the most powerful weapon which you can use to change the world.

Nelson Mandela

Equality

Whether it is unequal pay or unequal access to education for girls and women, equality is a pressing issue for all of us. In developing countries that are male dominated, women are treated as inferior and subservient and even as property.

Women's empowerment and women's inequality is the unfinished agenda of our time.

Fazle Hasan Adeb

Founder & Chairperson, BRAC

Lack of Resources

Every child should have access to school. However, in some areas of the world, earning an education is nearly impossible for girls and women. In some cases, there are no schools in their villages; there are not enough trained teachers available, and parents have no money to pay for school fees, uniforms, and materials. With limited resources, parents often decide to send their boys to school while girls are responsible for household chores.

For example, girls born in Yemen suffer from a very high illiteracy rate. In Pakistan, only 42 percent of girls and women know how to read and only 16 percent of Ethiopian girls attend secondary school (UNICEF, 2013).

Girls are the future mothers of any society. Every girl that receives an education is more likely to make education a priority for her children. It's a ripple effect of positive change in the community and country.

Tariq Al Gurg

Chief Executive Officer

Dubai Cares

Rights

In the developing world, girls and women are often denied the same rights as men. Whether it is a result of old patriarchal belief systems or the underrepresentation of women in positions of power – women are not treated equality. But the world is changing – and more women are demanding equality for all women. Education and awareness have played an important role is spurring the women's right movement all around the world. Kristof and WuDunn point out that education is "the single most important way to encourage women and girls to stand up for their rights."

Illiteracy can be a heavy barrier for underprivileged women. When a woman cannot read or write she is less likely to utilize the rights she may have, such as owning property or filing a police report. Education empowers women to exercise their legal rights against unfair treatment. Education is the pathway to empowerment. For every year a girl spends in school her chances of independence, economic freedom, and self-respect increase. And for every year girls spend in school, they are better able to advocate for themselves in their lives and relationships.

Minds will open, communities will strengthen, and slowly but surely, education will bring peace.

Central Asia Institute

Empowerment

Educating girls can change the trajectory of their lives. An education can mean the difference between living a life of dependency and living a life of hope and purpose.

In Saudi Arabia, for example, many women never get to experience an independent life. From the time they are born, girls are considered lifelong dependents of their male relatives. Saudi women are not allowed to drive and were only recently given the right to vote. Furthermore, they are required by law to be covered from top to bottom in public and cannot leave their homes unless escorted by a male relative. A woman traveling with a man who is not her husband, sponsor, or relative can be arrested.

Education empowers girls and leads to more opportunities to make decisions about their own lives. With an education, girls begin to understand their value, learn about their rights, participate in household decision making, and become less intimidated. For every year a girl spends in school, she becomes stronger and more independent.

Educating girls should be on the forefront of everyone's agenda. Obtaining an education is a pathway to economic and social freedom. Society places significant burdens on girls and women that can only be eradicated through access to education. Educating girls empowers us all and enhances the perspectives involving all disciplines and practices. We must educate girls.

LaShaila Spivey

J.D. Candidate, 2019

Maurer School of Law

The greatest threat to extremism isn't drones firing missiles, but girls reading books.

Nicholas Kristof

When girls have equal access to quality education... cycles of poverty are broken and economies grow.

www.clintonfoundation.org

ORGANIZATIONS

EDUCATING

GIRLS

ORGANIZATIONS EDUCATING GIRLS

The word is out - girls' education is a priority!

There has been major progress worldwide to close the gender gap in education. More girls have access to good schools; girls are enrolling and staying in school longer, and education standards are improving. Since 1990, the global movement for girls' education has been gaining momentum worldwide. Be it grassroots campaigns or multinational initiatives, the topic of girls' education has exploded.

Organizations

Girls' education organizations play an instrumental role in ensuring that girls around the world have access to schools. We are all thankful for the organizations that contribute to the empowerment and development of girls and women.

At every level - global, national, state, and local - hundreds of programs are working toward this same goal:

Educate Girls Around the World

This book is a tribute to the organizations that make the global movement for girls' education possible.

In this chapter, you'll learn about programs that teach girls around the world how to read and write, provide safe access to education, fundraise, advocate, build schools, train teachers, reform governments, mobilize communities, fund scholarships, support families, provide supplies, improve learning, and empower girls.

Because of the hard work of these phenomenal organizations, girls and women are in better health while being less likely to be victims of violence, human trafficking and child marriage. Their overall well-being has improved as has their personal wealth thanks to better employment opportunities due to equality and empowerment. **These organizations change lives!**

1.

60 Million Girls

5745 Place Turcot

Montreal, Quebec H4C 1W1

Website: 60millionsdefilles.org

Email: info@60milliongirls.org

Mission:

60 Million Girls is dedicated to girls' education and aims to support at least two major education-related projects in developing countries every year.

Service Locations:

Sierra Leone, Uganda, Nicaragua, Afghanistan, Kenya, Ethiopia, Indonesia, Democratic Republic of Congo, Côte d'Ivoire, Malawi, India, Zimbabwe, Honduras, and Zambia

2.

Afghan Institute of Learning

USA - ℅ CHI

P.O. Box 1058

Dearborn, Michigan 48121

Website: www.afghaninstituteoflearning.org

Email: sakena@afghaninstituteoflearning.org

Phone: 313-278-5806

Mission:

Afghan Institute of Learning provides education, training and health services to vulnerable Afghans in order to foster self-reliance, critical thinking skills, and community participation

Service Locations:

Afghanistan and Pakistan

3.

Akili Dada

1025 Alameda de las Pulgas, Number 310

Belmont, California 94002

Website: sites.google.com/site/akilidada

Email: info@akilidada.org

Phone: 650-592-2535

Kenya Address:

Hazina Towers, 16th Floor

P.O. Box 27847-00100

Nairobi

Phone: 254-721-552120

Mission:

Akili Dada works to empower the next generation of African women leaders by providing young women from underprivileged backgrounds access to high quality education, personalized mentoring, and rigorous leadership development.

4.

Asian University for Women Support Foundation

1100 Massachusetts Avenue

Cambridge, Massachusetts 02138

Website: www.asian-university.org

Phone: 1-617-914-0500

Mission:

The Asian University for Women seeks to graduate women who will be skilled and innovative professionals, service-oriented leaders, and promoters of intercultural understanding and sustainable human and economic development in Asia and throughout the world.

Service Location:

Asian University for Women in Chittagong, Bangladesh

5.

A World at School

Theirworld

The Broadgate Tower

20 Primrose Street

London EC2A 2RS

United Kingdom

Website: www.theirworld.org

Phone: (44) 020 3116 2735

Mission:

A World at School was convened by Theirworld in 2013 as a way of coordinating campaigning on global education. The A World at School network includes the Global Youth Ambassadors, young people, non-governmental organizations, civil society, teachers, faith-based organizations, media and leading businesses, who all come together to drive action on global education.

6.

Batonga Foundation

2000 Massachusetts Avenue NW, First Floor

Washington, D.C. 20036

Website: www.batongafoundation.org

Email: info@batongafoundation.org

Phone: 202-510-7169

Mission:

The Batonga Foundation exists to empower young women and girls in Africa through secondary school and higher education. We aim to remove the obstacles that prevent or discourage girls from attending school so they can take the lead in transforming Africa.

The Batonga Foundation works to improve school infrastructure, increase enrollment, grant scholarships, provide in-kind support and micro loans for scholars' families, cultivate mentoring and tutoring programs, and advocate for community awareness of the value of education for girls.

7.

BRAC USA

110 William Street, 29th Floor

New York, New York 10038

Website: www.bracusa.org

Email: info@bracusa.org

Phone: 212-808-5615

Mission:

The BRAC mission is to empower people and communities in situations of poverty, illiteracy, disease and social injustice. Our interventions aim to achieve large scale, positive changes through economic and social programs that enable men and women to realize their potential.

Service Locations:

Bangladesh, Afghanistan, Pakistan, Tanzania, Uganda, South Sudan, Sierra Leone, Liberia, Myanmar, Nepal, and Philippines

8.

buildOn

P.O. Box 16741

Stamford, CT 06905

Website: www.buildon.org

Email: info@buildon.org

Twitter: @buildon

Mission:

The buildOn mission is to break the cycle of poverty, illiteracy and low expectations through service and education. buildOn empowers urban youth to transform their neighborhoods through intensive community service and to change the world by building schools in some of the economically poorest countries in the world.

Service Locations:

Burkina Faso, Haiti, Mali, Malawi, Nepal, Nicaragua, and Senegal; US Regions: Chicago, Detroit, New York, the Bay Area, Boston, and Bridgeport, and Connecticut.

9.

Cambodian Children's Fund

P.O. Box 111

Phnom Pehn

Cambodia

Website: www.cambodianchildrensfund.org

Email: info@cambodianchildrensfund.org

Phone: +855(0)23 988 999

Mission:

The Cambodian Children's Fund transforms the country's most impoverished kids into tomorrow's leaders, by delivering education, family support and community development programs into the heart of Cambodia's most impoverished communities.

10.

Campaign for Female Education (Camfed)

St. Giles Court

24 Castle Street

Cambridge, CB3 0AJ

United Kingdom

Website: www.camfed.org

Email: info@camfed.org

Phone: 0044 (0) 1223-362-648

U.S. Address:

Camfed USA

465 California Street, Suite 626

San Francisco, California 94104

Email: usa@camfed.org

Phone: 415-963-4489

Mission:

The mission of Camfed is to eradicate poverty in Africa through the education of girls and the empowerment of young women.

Service Locations:

Zimbabwe, Zambia, Ghana, Tanzania, and Malawi

11.

CARE

151 Ellis Street, NE

Atlanta, Georgia 30303

Website: www.care.org

Email: info@care.org

Phone: 800-422-7385

Twitter: @care

#stealthesestats

Mission:

CARE works around the globe to save lives, defeat poverty, and achieve social justice. They create powerful education initiatives that are crucial to fighting poverty.

12.

Catapult

77 Sands Street, 6th Floor

New York, New York 11201

Website: www.catapult.org

Phone: 718-749-9545

Twitter: @wecatapult

Mission:

Catapult is a crowdfunding platform where people can join forces for a more equal world. 100 percent of donations support projects for women and girls' equality and rights.

Donate and support a girls' education project today!

13.

Central Asia Institute

P.O. Box 7209

Bozeman, Montana 59771

Website: www.centralasiainstitute.org

Email: info@centralasiainstitute.org

Phone: 877-585-7841

#BeHerHero

Mission:

Founded by *Three Cups of Tea* author Greg Mortenson, Central Asia Institute promotes and supports community-based education, especially for girls

Service Locations:

Afghanistan, Pakistan, and Tajikistan

Educating one woman is the equivalent of educating several men because she shares her knowledge with her family, her children, and her community, amplifying the impact of one school ten-fold.

www.centralasiainstitute.org

14.

Circle of Sisterhood

P.O. Box 90257

Indianapolis, IN 46290

Website: www.circleofsisterhood.org

Email: info@circleofsisterhood.org

Phone: 317-775-9488

Mission:

The Circle of Sisterhood will leverage the collective influence of sorority women to raise financial resources for entities around the world that are removing educational barriers for girls and women facing poverty and oppression.

Service Locations:

United States and developing countries

15.

The Clinton Foundation –

Collaborative for Harnessing Ambition and Resources for Girls' Education (CHARGE)

1271 Avenue of the Americas, 42nd Floor

New York, New York 10020

Website: www.clintonfoundation.org

Phone: 212-348-8882

Twitter: @Clintonfnd

Mission:

In 2014, the Center for Universal Education at the Brookings Institution committed to bring together leading public, private, and civil society organizations from across the globe that focused on advancing solutions in girls' education that have the greatest potential for sustainable impact. Through the Collaborative Harnessing Ambition & Resources for Girls Education initiative, partner organizations will align individual efforts for improving girls' education to five research-informed priorities: (1) Access; (2) Safety; (3) Learning; (4) Transitions; and (5) Leadership.

16.

Commit2Change

500 West 23rd Street, Apt. 3D

New York, New York 10011

Website: www.commit2change.org

Email: info@commit2change.org

Phone: 914-715-0808

#sheisthefuture

Mission:

Commit2Change works to educate abandoned and impoverished girls in India's orphanages. Commit2Change works with carefully selected local partners who rescue and rehabilitate at-risk girls and invest in initiatives to give them a chance.

17.

Developments in Literacy

17320 Red Hill Avenue, Suite 120

Irvine, CA 92614

Website: www.dil.org

Email: office@dil.org

Phone: 949-474-5303

Mission:

Developments in Literacy educates and empowers disadvantaged children, especially girls, by operating schools in the underdeveloped regions of Pakistan.

18.

Educate a Child

Education Above All Foundation

MB-3 Building

Education City

P.O. Box 34173

Doha-Qatar

Website: www.educateachild.org

Email: info@educateachild.org.qa

Mission:

Educate a Child works with partner organizations to trigger significant breakthroughs in providing out of school children faced with extreme poverty, cultural barriers, and conflict-affected environments an opportunity for a full course of quality primary education.

19.

Educate Girls Globally

5178 Mowry Avenue, Suite 144

Fremont, CA 94538

Website: www.educategirls.org

Email: info@educategirls.org

Mission:

The mission of Educate Girls Globally is to empower all major stakeholders to reform government schools and promote economic and social change even in the most traditional and tribal communities.

Educating girls [is] one of the best and most cost-effective ways to spur development. It is positively correlated with increased economic productivity, more robust labor markets, higher earnings and improved societal health and well-being.

World Bank

www.worldbank.org

20.

Educate Girls /

Foundation to Educate Girls Globally (FEGG)

201, Durolite House, Opp.

City Mall, New Link Road

Andheri West, Mumbai 400053

Website: www.educategirls.in

Website: www.educategirls.ngo

Email: info.in@educategirls.ngo

Facebook: www.facebook.com/educategirls

Phone: +91-22 2630 3555

Twitter: @educate_girls

Mission:

Educate Girls leverages existing community and government resources to ensure that all girls are in school and learning well.

21.

EMpower

Emerging Markets Foundation

111 John Street, Suite 2410

New York, New York 10038

Website: www.empowerweb.org

Email: empowerus@empowerweb.org

Phone: 212-608-4455

London Address:

c/o Finisterre Capital

10 New Burlington Street

London W1S 3BE

Email: empoweruk@empowerweb.org

Hong Kong Address:

9A Foo Cheong Building

82-86 Wing Lok Street Sheung Wan

Hong Kong

Email: empowerhk@empowerweb.org

Mission:

EMpower is a global philanthropic organization that connects the resources of Emerging Markets professionals worldwide with the vitality of local organizations in emerging market countries. EMpower develops partnerships with local community-based organizations in EM countries, working to improve the lives of at-risk young people as well as to create communities where all youth can thrive.

22.

Forum for African Women Educationalists

FAWE House

Chania Avenue, Off Wood Avenue Kilimani

P.O. Box 21394-00505

Ngong Road

Nairobi, Kenya

Website: www.fawe.org

Email: fawe@fawe.org

Phone: +254 20 77 30537

Mission:

Forum for African Women Educationalists (FAWE) is a pan-African Non-Governmental Organization working in 33 African countries to empower girls and women through gender-responsive education.

23.

The Freedom Project

Formally known as The SOLD Project

19 Collins Road

St. Ives, NSW 2075

Website: www.thefreedomproject.org

Email: info@thefreedomproject.org

Phone: 1300 373 363

Mission:

Through the Freedom Project, children are rescued, rehabilitated, educated and prevented from being trafficked.

Service Locations:

India, Thailand, Philippines, and Burma

24.

Girl Determined

77 Dhamazedi Road

Sanchaung Township

Yangon, Yangon 11111

Myanmar

Website: www.girldetermined.org

Phone: 959-545-001-5996

Mission:

Girl Determined is a leadership project designed to assist girls ages 12-17 to avoid the pitfalls of trafficking, dangerous labor and other forms of violence, by facilitating girls' recognition of their personal and group potential. The program aims to increase girls' ability to make strategic life-decisions, generate choices and exercise bargaining power.

Service Location:

Myanmar

Photo by Ten Times Ten LLC, provided by GIRL RISING © 2013

25.

Girl Rising

P.O. Box 537

Boulder, Colorado 80306-0537

Website: www.girlrising.com

Mission:

Girl Rising is a global campaign for girls' education and empowerment.

Film:

Girl Rising (2014)

Produced by M. Adams

This film tells the stories of nine unforgettable girls fighting to be educated.

Book:

Girl Rising: Changing the World One Girl at a Time (2017)

By Tanya Lee Stone

Educate Girls Around The World

Photo provided by Girls Education International

26.

Girls Education International

P.O. Box 537

Boulder, Colorado 80306-0537

Website: www.girlsed.org

Email: info@girlsed.org

Facebook: www.facebook.com/GirlsEd

Mission:

The mission of girls' education International is to increase access to education for girls and women in remote underserved regions of the world. They accomplish this through educational programming with nongovernmental organization partners in Pakistan and Tanzania.

Girls Education International's contribution is simple. They partner with nonprofit entities in other countries and support them in their work to educate and empower girls and young women. In Pakistan, that includes programming to take the girls on excursions throughout the country to teach them about the history, geography, art, and environment of their nation. These experiences outside of the home in the company of peers and educators has really built up their self-confidence and sense of connection to their country. In Tanzania, the programming for girls in the villages includes participation in rigorous academic study camps between semesters and tutoring support throughout the school year as needed.

Education gives them a chance at making better life decisions, getting better jobs, becoming an active part of their communities, and being part of the momentum in moving their country towards a stable civil society.

Girls Education International

Photo provided by Girls Education International

Educate a woman, you educate a nation.

-Phumzile Mlambo-Ngcuka

Deputy President 4th Annual Women's Parliament

Conference

27.

GirlsHelpingGirls

1300 Don Mills Road, Suite 203

North York, Ontario M3B 2W6

Canada

Website: www.girlshelpinggirls.ca

Email: susanna@girlshelpinggirls.ca

Mission:

GirlsHelpingGirls works to raise the status of women through education and has three objectives: to build schools to support a healthy and stimulating learning environment; to provide teachers with the proper training and resources so they can best support their students; and to create scholarships for students to go to school.

Service Locations:

Jamaica, Afghanistan, South Africa, and Kenya.

28.

Girls Learn International, Inc.

1600 Wilson Boulevard, Suite 801

Arlington, VA 22209

Website: www.girlslearn.org

Twitter: @GirlsLearnIntl

Phone: 703-522-2214

Mission:

Girls Learn International educates and energizes students in the global movement for girls' access to education. The Girls Learn International Program supports the empowerment of students as they discover that through their own creative initiatives, dedication, and passionate leadership, they can create real solutions that address the obstacles facing girls and women in the U.S. and around the world.

Girls Learn International is building a movement of informed advocates for universal girls' education and a new generation of leaders and activists for social change.

29.

Global Campaign for Education

The Education Hub

6 Blackwood Avenue

Parkstown, Johannesburg

2193, South Africa

Website: www.campaignforeducation.org

Email: info@campaignforeducation.org

Mission:

The Global Campaign for Education is a civil society movement whose mission is to make sure that governments act now to deliver the right of every girl and boy to a free, quality public education. The Global Campaign for Education brings together NGO's teacher unions, child rights activists, and community organizations in 100 countries to realize the right of everyone to free, quality education.

Service Locations:

Over 120 national coalitions and international and regional organizations.

30.

Global Partnership for Education

℅ World Bank

MSN IS6-600

1818 H Street NW

Washington, D.C. 20433

Website: www.globalpartnership.org

Email: information@globalpartnership.org

Phone: 202-522-3923

Mission:

Global Partnership for Education is a multi-stakeholder partnership and funding platform that galvanizes global and national support for education in 65 developing countries, focusing on the poorest and most vulnerable children and youth.

31.

Going to School

Website: www.goingtoschool.com

Email: mail@goingtoschool.com

Phone: 011 41739945

Mission:

Going to School creates design-driven stories to teach the poorest kids on the planet 21st century skills at school.

Service Locations:

Going to School operates across 10 states in India.

32.

Graca Machel Trust

Hyde Park Lane

Victoria Gate South

Johannesburg, 2196

South Africa

Website: www.gracamacheltrust.org

Email: info@gracamacheltrust.org

Phone: 27 (0) 11 325 0501

Mission:

Graca Machel Trust amplifies women's movements, influence governance and promote women's contributions and leadership in the economic, social and political development of Africa; and advocate for the protection of children's rights and dignity.

Photo provided by HURU International

33.

HURU International

15 West 26th Street, 11th Floor

New York, New York 10010

Website: www.huruinternational.org

Email: info@huruinternational.org

Phone: 212-340-7115

Facebook: www.facebook.com/HuruKits

Twitter: @HuruKits

Instagram: instagram.com/hurukits

Mission:

Huru International is a nonprofit organization that provides at-risk girls in Africa with reusable sanitary pads combined with sexual and reproductive health and life skills workshops so that they can stay in school and remain healthy. Unable to afford sanitary protection, many young women in Africa use dangerous alternatives like used pads, pieces of mattress, or cow dung to manage their periods. Others engage in transactional sex to obtain sanitary protection. Many girls skip school completely or fail to fully participate in class during their periods, which causes insurmountable academic gaps and can lead them to abandon their studies altogether. Girls end up falling behind in their studies or dropping out of school, perpetuating the vicious cycles of gender inequality and poverty that exist on the continent.

Huru believes educated young women are essential to Africa's success and has produced more than 1,000,000 pads that have been distributed to 120,000 girls in Kenya and Tanzania.

Photo provided by HURU International

Our vision at Huru is for a world where no girl misses school because of her period.

Emily Hoppes

Program Director and Partner Liaison

Huru International

34.

IIMPACT

M – 2/3, Ground Floor

DLF City Phase II

Gurgaon, Haryana – 122002

India

Website: www.iimpact.org

Email: info@iimpact.org

Phone: +91 124 4276865 – 67

Mission:

IIMPACT's mission is to mobilize and motivate non-school going girls, between the ages of 6 and 14, from economically and socially backward rural areas of India, and put them firmly on the track of literacy through quality primary education. IIMPACT is an initiative of alumni of the Indian Institute of Management, Ahmedabad, India.

Service Locations:

India

Educate Girls Around The World

Photo provided by Girls Education International

35.

Irise International

3 The Holt

Purley on Thames

Reading RG8 8HZ

United Kingdom

Website: www.irise.org.uk

Phone: +44 (0) 7519459582

Twitter: @irise_intl

Uganda Address:

P.O. Box 1237

Plot 4

Lubogo Lane

Jinja

Phone +256 (0) 781966521

Mission:

Irise International works to support the education and empowerment of marginalized women and girls in East Africa specifically through developing a replicable and sustainable solution to Menstrual Hygiene Management (MHM).

36.

Let Girls Learn

Website: letgirlslearn.gov

Email: letgirlslearn@usaid.gov

#LetGirlsLearn

Mission:

In March 2015, President Obama and First Lady Michelle Obama launched Let Girls Learn to address the range of challenges preventing adolescent girls from attaining a quality education that empowers them to reach their full potential.

Partners:

-U.S. Department of State

-U.S. Agency for International Development (USAID)

-Peace Corps

-U.S. Department of Labor

-U.S. Department of Agriculture

-Millennium Challenge Corporation (MCC)

-U.S. President's Emergency Fund for AIDS Relief (PEPFAR)

Educate Girls Around The World

I see myself in these girls, I see my daughters in these girls, and I simply cannot walk away from them.

Michelle Obama

Former First Lady of the United States

37.

The Malala Fund

P.O. Box 53347

Washington, D.C. 20009

Website: www.malala.org

Twitter: @MalalaFund

Mission:

The Malala Fund advocates at local, national, and international levels for resources and policy changes needed to ensure all girls complete 12 years of school.

Service Locations:

Pakistan, Nigeria, Lebanon, Jordan, Syrian, Sierra Leone, Kenya, and Nairobi

38.

Mama Cash

P.O. Box 15686

1001 ND Amsterdam, The Netherlands

Website: www.mamacash.org

Email: info@mamacash.org

Phone: +31 20-5158-700

Mission:

Each year, Mama Cash provides approximately 100 grants to groups, organizations, and networks led by and working for the human rights of women, girls, and transgender people - including girls' education initiatives.

Service Locations:

Asia, Africa, the Middle East, Europe, Latin America and the Caribbean, and the Commonwealth of Independent States

39.

Massai Girls' Education Fund

5800 MacArthur Boulevard, NW

Washington D.C. 20016-2512

Website: maasaigirlseducation.org

Email: hmckay@maasaigirlseducation.org

Phone: 202-237-0536

Twitter: @MaasaiGirlsEduc

#literacyday

Mission:

The Maasai Girls' Education Fund's mission is to improve the literacy, health and economic well-being of Maasai women and their families in Kenya through the education of girls and their communities.

Service Location:

Kenya

40.

Mona Foundation

218 Main Street, #404

Kirkland, WA 98033

Website: www.monafoundation.org

Email: info@monafoundation.org

Phone: 425-743-4550

Mission:

Mona Foundation supports grassroots educational initiatives and raises the status of women and girls across the world.

41.

Mercy Corps

45 SW Ankeny Street

Portland, Oregon 97208-2669

Website: www.mercycorps.org

Phone: 800-292-3355

Mission:

Mercy Corps mission is to alleviate suffering, poverty and oppression by helping people build secure, productive and just communities.

Mercy Corps works to bring access to education to women and men of all ages and economic.

Photo provided by Girls Education International

Every girl empowered

More Than Me Foundation, Inc.

www.morethanme.org

42.

More Than Me Foundation, Inc.

P.O. Box 438

Bernardsville, New Jersey 07924

Website: www.morethanme.org

Email: hi@morethanme.org

Phone: 415-343-5632

Mission:

More Than Me uses education as a catalyst for transformative social change for every girl in Liberia.

43.

Mukhtar Mai Women's Organization

Mukhtar Mai School for Girls

Mukhtar Mai Women's Organization

Mouza Meerwala

Tehsil Jatoi, District Muzaffargarh

Punjab Pakistan

Website: www.mukhtarmai.org

Mission:

The Mukhtar Mai Women's Organization envisions an equal opportunity society where men and women are treated equally and are able to exercise their civil, political, social, economic and cultural rights.

The Mukhtar Mai Women's Organization is committed to work against all forms of violence and discrimination against women through advocacy, capacity building, awareness raising and service delivery at all levels of society.

The Mukhtar Mai Women's Organization is aspiring to bring about positive and lasting change by provisions of services that promotes economic, social and cultural empowerment.

The Mukhtar Mai Women's Organization is working to eliminate violence against women through education, advocacy, capacity building, awareness raising, and service delivery at all levels of society.

The Mukhtar Mai Girl's Model School provides free education, with free books, supplies, and uniforms to over 550 girls from nursery school to grade 10.

44.

Oprah Winfrey Leadership Academy for Girls - South Africa

534 Wargrave Road

Meyerton, 1961, South Africa

Website: www.owla.co.za

Phone: +27 16 366 9000

Mission:

The Oprah Winfrey Leadership Academy for Girls strives to provide a nurturing educational environment for academically gifted girls who come from disadvantaged backgrounds. Our educational programs are designed for girls in Grades 8 to 12 who have demonstrated academic talent and leadership potential.

They equip students with the intellectual and social skills necessary to assume positions of leadership in South Africa and abroad.

45.

Pencils of Promise

37 West 28th Street, 3rd Floor

New York, New York 10001

Website: www.pencilsofpromise.org

Email: team@pencilsofpromise.org

Phone: 212-777-3170

Mission:

Pencils of Promise is a global education organization that believes every child should have access to quality education. Pencils of Promise creates schools, programs, and global communities with the common goal of education for all.

Service Locations:

Ghana, Guatemala, Laos, and Nicaragua.

46.

Plan International USA

155 Plan Way

Warwick, Rhode Island 02886

Website: www.cedpa.org

Phone: 401-562-8400

Washington, D.C. Office:

1255 23rd Street NW, Suite 300

Washington, D.C. 20037

Phone 202-617-2300

Mission:

Plan International USA works in partnership with local leaders and organizations to provide girls with practical, non-formal education in countries around the world.

Service Locations:

Plan International USA works in more than 50 countries around the world.

47.

Save the Children - Education

501 Kings Highway East, Suite 400

Fairfield, Connecticut 06825

Website: www.savethechildren.org

Phone: 203-221-4000

#everylastgirl

Mission:

Save the Children's mission is to inspire breakthroughs in the way the world treats children and to achieve immediate and lasting change in their lives.

Save the Children supports education programs around the world for children in the classroom and at home.

48.

School the World

376 Boylston Street, Suite 203

Boston, MA 02116

Website: www.schooltheworld.org

Email: info@schooltheworld.org

Phone: 617-867-9500

Mission:

School the World is a nonprofit organization founded on the belief that empowerment begins with education. They provide access to quality education for those living in the rural villages of Central America.

Service Location:

Central America

49.

Shining Hope for Communities

P.O. Box 8303-00200

Gatwakera, Kibera

Website: www.shofco.org

Phone: +254-732058126

New York Address:

175 Varick Street, 6th Floor

New York, New York 10014

Phone: 860-218-9854

Mission:

Shining Hope for Communities combats gender inequality and extreme poverty in urban slums by linking tuition free schools for girls to holistic social services for all.

Service Locations:

Nairobi, Kibera, and Mathare

50.

The TARA Project

Website: taraproject.org

Email: info@taraproject.org

Phone: 706-238-0860

Twitter: @TaraProject

Mission:

The TARA Project's mission is to improve access to health, education and economic opportunity for chronically poor communities. They provide scholarships for secondary school and university in Kenya. They research hygiene solutions to increase girls' regular attendance in school. They also partner with local schools to identify other ways to provide a safe, well-equipped learning space.

51.

Tererai Trent International

P.O. Box 2206

Salinas, California 93901

Website: tererai.org

Email: info@tt-international.org

Phone: 831-382-3009

Twitter: @TereraiTrent

Zimbabwe Address:

18 Fletcher Road, Mount Pleasant

Harare, Zimbabwe

Phone +263 4 301 579

Mission:

Tererai Trent International's mission is to lead the development and growth of an improved education system supported by socially engaged business models that boost local economies while improving community livelihoods.

Service Location:

Zimbabwe

52.

United Nations Education, Scientific and Cultural Organization (UNESCO)

7 Place Fontenoy

75007 Paris, France

Website: www.unesco.org

Phone: +33 (0)1 4568 1000

Mission:

United Nations Education, Scientific and Cultural Organization (UNESCO) contributes to the building of peace, the eradication of poverty, sustainable development and intercultural dialogue through education, the sciences, culture, communication and information.

In girls' education, UNESCO strives to build networks among nations that enable solidarity by mobilizing for education.

Service Locations:

UNESCO has over 50 field offices and 90 specialized institutes and centers around the world.

53.

United Nations Girls' Education Initiative (UNGEI)

3 United Nations Plaza

New York, New York 10017

Website: www.ungei.org

Mission:

The United Nations Girls' Education Initiative (UNGEI) is committed to accelerating action on girls' education to realize "A world where all girls and boys are empowered through quality education to realize their full potential and contribute to transforming societies where gender equality becomes a reality."

Service Locations:

East Asia and the Pacific, Eastern and Southern Africa, the Middle East and North Africa, South Asia, and West and Central Africa.

54.

United Nations Women - Fund for Gender Equality

220 East 42nd Street

New York, New York 10017

Website: www.unwomen.org

Phone: 646-781-4400

Mission:

The Fund for Gender Equality is UN Women's global grantmaking mechanism dedicated to the economic and political empowerment of women worldwide. Guided by UN Women's mandate, the Fund provides technical and financial support to high-impact, innovative initiatives from women-led civil society organizations that demonstrate concrete results on the ground, especially for women in situations of marginalization.

55.

Vital Voices

1625 Massachusetts Avenue, NW, Suite 300

Washington, D.C. 20036

Website: www.vitalvoices.org

Email: info@vitalvoices.org

Twitter: @vitalvoices

Mission:

Vital Voices mission is to identify, invest in and bring visibility to extraordinary women around the world by unleashing their leadership potential to transform lives and accelerate peace and prosperity in their communities.

Service Locations:

Africa, Asia, Eurasia, Latin America, the Caribbean, the Middle East, and North Africa.

56.

Women's Institute of Secondary Education & Research / WISER International (WISER)

P.O. Box 3186

Durham, North Carolina 27715

Website: www.wisergirls.org

Email: wiser@wisergirls.org

Twitter: @WISER_Intl

Mission:

The Women's Institute of Secondary Education & Research (WISER) works to improve the health and educational outcomes for girls, particularly those orphaned by AIDS. WISER also works with the community to change how girls are valued and provide community programs.

Service Location:

Kenya

57.

World Assistance for Cambodia and Japan Relief for Cambodia

P.O. Box 2716 GPO

New York, New York 10116

Website: www.cambodiaschools.com

Email: Bernie@media.mit.edu

Phone: 212-658-9419

Japan Address:

4-1-7 605 Hiroo

Shibuya-ku, Tokyo (150-10012)

Japan

Mission:

World Assistance for Cambodia / Japan Relief for Cambodia is an independent, nonprofit organization dedicated to improving opportunities for the youth and rural poor in Cambodia. They operate programs across Cambodia in the areas of education, health, rural development, and technology.

Educate Girls Around The World

Cambodian girl

Photo by © Martha Adams, 10x10act.org, provided by GIRL RISING
© 2013

Be the Change.

Educating girls can break the cycle of poverty.

WHAT

YOU

CAN

DO

TO

HELP

WHAT YOU CAN DO TO HELP

This is where you come in.

Support girls' education. Join the movement!

Donate Money

Your donations are needed to help organizations that are working to educate girls. There are several organizations at work in the communities that need it most, but they need help to stay there. I encourage you to choose an organization that speaks to your heart and make a tax-deductible donation.

Donation Examples:

- Afghan Institute of Learning has a Global Giving page where you can choose a project and donate to it. For example, $32 will give four girls the chance to attend a computer class; $10 will buy two books for a library; and $15 can help train a teacher.

- Choose to donate to Camfed and provide a girl with school supplies, new shoes, or a school uniform.

- Your donation of $17 to CARE can provide a girl with her own school kit, which includes a bag, notebooks, pencils, and hygiene items. $75 can supply a year's worth of drinking water and sanitation for 25 students.

- Support a girls' education project on Catapult, a crowd funding platform. 100 percent of donations support projects for women and girls' rights and equality.

- All donations to The Freedom Project over $2 are fully tax deductible and tax receipts are automatically emailed to you when you donate online.

- Helping Huru is simple. A $35 donation will keep a girl in school while managing her menstrual period with dignity.

- The Malala Fund will donate 100 percent of your donation to local Nigerian nonprofit organizations focused on education and advocacy for girls and women.

- At Room to Read, a donation from you can provide a girl with a mentor, safe transportation to school, a uniform, and supplies.

- A $70 gift to Save the Children can educate a girl, giving her everything she needs to succeed in school.

- Donate to Shining Hope for Communities and sponsor a student's education at the Kibera School for Girls.

Donate Your Time

Volunteer!

Many organizations are looking for volunteers to help build awareness, complete daily tasks and tackle specialty assignments. I hope you consider sharing your special talents.

You can volunteer from home or contact an organization and arrange a visit in person. Your life will never be the same!

Raise Awareness - Host a Film Viewing

Organize and host a film screening in your area to raise awareness and understanding about the issue of educating girls around the world.

- *Half the Sky: Turning Oppression into Opportunity for Women Worldwide* (M. Chermayeff, producer)
- *Girl Rising* (M. Adams, producer)
- *It's a Girl* (A. Brown, producer)

Raise Awareness - Organize a Local TEDx Event

A TEDx event is a local gathering where live TED-like talks and videos previously recorded at TED conferences are shared with the community. More information at www.ted.com

Share the stories to multiply the impact.

A simple action that many people can take to make an impact on girls' education around the

world is to become aware of the barriers that many girls face to accessing education, and then raise awareness about these issues within your spheres of influence.

Joy Lynn Alegarbes

Director of Community

Huru International

Raise Awareness - Share to Social Media

Become part of the movement!

You can share this book, a moving video, or a written piece about the global movement for girls' education to help raise awareness. The more people that know - the better. Get creative by posting a picture of your support on Facebook, Twitter, Instagram, LinkedIn, etc.

Collaborate

Don't be afraid to reach out and ask how you can help (i.e "What does your organization need? How can I be of service?").

Help support girls' education by hosting a fundraising event for a worthwhile organization. For example, Adam Braun, the founder of Pencils of Promise, would throw parties to raise money for his favorite organization.

Collaborative fundraising initiatives begin when groups come together to raise funds, awareness, and materials, or to share potential solutions for a problem. For example, a school club can host a sock drive to collect socks for a local homeless organization. Some organizations raise funds to help other organizations build schools in a developing country. In the case of girls' education, your school could host a book drive to donate books to an organization in need.

> *We really welcome collaborative fundraising initiatives like students for students, schools for schools. I am very keen on guiding classes through the early stages of launching their own fundraising campaigns for our programs, so if there are any teachers out there who would like to collaborate, please be in touch!*
>
> Raichle Farrelly
> Executive Director
> Girls' Education International

Partner Up!

> *... it is also important and useful to connect with people working in other countries for girls' education, to establish connections between girls in your area and those in third world countries. Initiatives such as setting up partnerships between schools across different cultures and languages have also proved useful for developing global understanding.*

Judith Gill PhD

Adjunct A/Professor of Education

University of South Australia

#EVERYLASTGIRL

STATEMENT FROM THE AUTHOR

STATEMENT FROM THE AUTHOR

I stand for girls and support the global movement for girls' education.

Yes, the problems are many, but change is happening, and this book is part of the fight for the right of all girls to have equal access to education.

Girls around the world need each and every one of us to speak up for equality for everyone:

- Equal rights
- Equal access
- Equal opportunity
- Equal treatment
- Equal status
- Equal pay
- Equal power
- Equal say

While this book outlines issues and organizations specific to girls and women, educating girls will positively impact everyone - men, women, girls, and boys around the world. Girls' education has a global impact! Equality is long overdue. I vote against the cultural norms that say that girls are in anyway inferior or less valuable than boys.

While researching this book, I learned things that brought me to tears, but I also discovered good people doing good work. Girls around the world need united advocates in all areas of education and social justice. So, let's celebrate today's girls' education advocates. I am inspired by the organizations that are making a difference in global education - especially for girls. They may be the leaders in the girls' education movement, but they do not operate alone. They need us, so let's become good global citizens and do something – anything – to support the cause.

Let's build on the progress made, but never forget that there is more work left to be done. We want girls to stay in school longer and for those schools to be top-notch. We must close the gender gap in education and ensure that just as many girls attend school as boys. And until we reach this goal, we must continue to fight and educate.

Let's get involved. Raising awareness raises the chances of every little girl being a better woman. I want to raise awareness about issues girls and women face worldwide - especially education - and to stress the benefits education has when it comes to tearing down barriers.

My Background in Social Work

I went into social work to become a voice for the voiceless and to help the helpless. I have worked for years to promote equal access to education for disadvantaged students because I believe education is the key to success. And social work is the perfect field for social justice. Social workers are trained to help people address their problems and to match them with the resources they need to lead healthy and productive lives (NASW, 2017).

Why Girls' Education?

Girls' education holds a special place in my heart. First, because I'm a girl too! I am not a second class citizen or a piece of property because of my gender. Second, I want a better, more equal world for my daughters – for all our daughters. I gained a deeper understanding of the importance of girls' education after listening to Oprah Winfrey explain why she built her girls' school in Africa and after reading *Half the Sky: Turning Oppression into Opportunity for Women Worldwide*. It was all about systematic change. When a woman understands that she is worthy she will act accordingly.

CONTACT

SHAY

SPIVEY

CONTACT SHAY SPIVEY

Thank you for reading this book! I would love to receive your feedback. Also, feel free to share your thoughts about this book by leaving a review wherever you made your purchase.

Email:

shayspivey@yahoo.com

Scholarship Blog:

www.educategirlsaroundtheworld.blogspot.com

Author Blog:

www.shayspivey.blogspot.com

Facebook:

facebook.com/educategirlsaroundtheworld

Twitter:

@ShayMSpivey; #educategirlsaroundtheworld

Other Books by Shay Spivey

FREE Money for Education Series:
How to Submit a Winning Scholarship Application:
Secret Techniques I Used to Win $100,000 in College
Scholarships
How to Find Scholarships and Free Financial Aid for
Private High Schools
FREE Tuition Colleges 2016
Find FREE Money for Graduate School
FREE Tuition Colleges for Adults 50+
Understanding Scholarships and Financial Aid
Where to Find FREE Money for College

Prepare for College Series:
Prepare for College Series: The Complete Collection
Prepare for College: Middle School Checklist
Prepare for College: Freshman Year Checklist
Prepare for College: Sophomore Year Checklist
Prepare for College: Junior Year Checklist
Prepare for College: Senior Year Checklist

Quick Reference Series:
FREE Online College Courses for Everyone
FREE Online Art Courses
FREE Online Biology Courses
FREE Online Business Courses
FREE Online Computer Courses
FREE Online Economics Courses
FREE Online Engineering Courses
FREE Online History Courses

Educate Girls Around The World

FREE Online Law Courses
FREE Online Math Courses
FREE Online Philosophy Courses
FREE Online Psychology Courses
FREE Online State Programs

#BEHERHERO

RESOURCES

RESOURCES

Policies and Laws that Protect the Right to Education

- Universal Declaration on Human Rights in 1948

- International Covenant on Economic, Social and Cultural Rights (1966)

- Convention on the Elimination of Discrimination Against Women (1979)

- Convention on the Rights of the Child (1989)

- The Dakar Framework for Action, Education for All: Meeting our Collective Commitments. Adopted by the World Education Forum. Dakar, Senegal, April 2000.

- 1990 World Declaration of Education for All and Framework for Action to Meet Basic Learning Needs. Adopted by the World Conference on Education for All Meeting Basic Learning Needs. Jomtien, Thailand. March 1990.

Global Education Data Sources

The Brookings Institution
www.brookings.edu

The Global Education Monitoring Report
En.unesco.org/gem-report/reports

UNESCO Institute of Statistics
www.uis.unesco.org

The World Bank
Datatopics.worldbank.org/education/

United Nation's Leaders for Education in Emergencies

UNICEF

United Nations International Children's Emergency Fund

www.unicef.org

UNHCR

Office of the United Nations High Commissioner of Refugees

www.unhcr.org

Films

Half the Sky: Turning Oppression into Opportunity for Women Worldwide (2012)
Produced by Maro Chermayeff

Girl Rising (2014)
Produced M. Adams

It's a Girl (2012)
Produced by A. Brown

Campaigns and Organizations Working to Prevent Child Marriage:

- Every Woman Every Child
- Girls Not Brides
- Partnership for Maternal Newborn and Child Health
- United Nations Foundation
- UNFPA
- UNICEF
- UN Women
- World Vision
- World YMCA

REFERENCES

REFERENCES

Adams, M. (Producer), Robbins, R. E. (Producer), & Yellin, T. (Producer). (2014). *Girl Rising* [Motion Picture]. New York: 10x10 & The Documentary Group, Vulcan Productions, in association with CNN Films & Gathr, & Intel Corporation.

Academic Council on the United Nations System Vienna Liaison Office (2013). *Femicide: A global issue that demands action.* Retrieved from http://www.genevadeclaration.org/fileadmin/docs/Co-publications/Femicide_A percent20Gobal percent20Issue percent20that percent20demands percent20Action.pdf

Braun, A. (2014). *The promise of a pencil: How an ordinary person can create extraordinary change.* New York: Scribner

Brown, A. (Producer), & Davis, E. G. (Director). (2012). *It's a Girl* [Motion Picture]. United States: Shadowline Films.

Camfed Ghana. (2012). *What Works in Girls' Education in Ghana: A critical review of the Ghanaian and international literature.* Ghana Education Service, Department of Internal Development.

Chermayeff, M. (Executive Producer & Director), Beardsley, M. (Producer), Gordon, J. (Producer), Dupre, J. (Producer), & Bennett, J. (Producer). (2012). *Half the Sky: Turning oppression into opportunity for women worldwide* [Motion picture]. New York: Show of Force, LLC & Fugitive Films, LLC.

Constable, P. (2016). *In Pakistan, five girls were killed for having fun. Then the story took an even darker twist.* Retrieved from https://www.washingtonpost.com/world/in-pakistan-five-girls-were-killed-for-having-fun-then-the-story-took-an-even-darker-twist/2016/12/16/f2adbd5e-c13a-11e6-92e8-c07f4f671da4_story.html?tid=a_inl&utm_term=.260a4a440e09

Dorell, Oren. (2014). *Terrorists kidnap more than 200 Nigerian girls. USA Today*. Retrieved from http://www.usatoday.com/story/news/world/2014/0 4/21/parents-234-girls-kidnapped-from-nigeria-school/7958307/

Equality Now. (2017). *The world's shame: The global rape epidemic.*

Fong, M. (2016). One child: The story of China's most radical experiment. Houghton: Mifflin Harcourt.

Gannon, K. (2016). *In a Pakistan family, deal is made, a girl is given as bride*. Retrieved from https://www.washingtonpost.com/world/asia_pacific/i n-a-pakistan-family-deal-is-made-a-girl-is-given-as-bride/2016/12/30/1940c522-ce58-11e6-85cd-e66532e35a44_story.html?utm_term=.36e4c5edcf8b

Gill J., Esson K. & Yuen R. (2016). *A Girl's Education, Schooling and the formation of gender, Identities and Future Visions.* London: Palgrave Macmillan

Global Coalition to Protect Education from Attack. (2014). *Education under attack: 2014.* New York: Global Coalition to Protect Education from Attack.

Global Fund for Women. (2017). Retrieved from www.globalfundforwomen.org

Global Partnership for Education Secretariat. (2015). *15 Women leading the way for girls' education.* Retrieved from http://www.globalpartnership.org/blog/15-women-leading-way-girls-education

Gyesaw, N. Y. K. & Ankomah, A. (2013*). Experiences of pregnancy and motherhood among teenage mothers in a suburb of Accra, Guana: a qualitative study.* International Journal of Women's Health. 5: 773-780.

Husain, M. (2013). *Malala: The girl who was shot for going to school.* Retrieved from http://www.bbc.com/news/magazine-24379018)

King, E. and Winthrop, R. (2015). *Today's Challenges for Girls' Education.* Washington: Brookings Institution.

Kristof, N. D. & WuDunn, S. (2009). *Half the Sky: Turning oppression into opportunity for women worldwide.* New York: Alfred A. Knopf.

Kristof, N. D. & WuDunn, S. (2014). *A path appears: Transforming lives, creating opportunity.* United States: Vintage Books.

Let Girls Learn. (2017). Retrieved from www.letgirlslearn.gov

Let Girls Learn. (2017). Retrieved from https://yali.state.gov/wp-content/uploads/sites/4/2016/03/USAID_LGL_FactSheet.pdf

Mitchell C. & Walsh, J. R. (2012). *The Time of the Girl.* Girlhood Studies Editorial, 5(2) 1-7

Mohsin, S. & Schwarz, T. (2013). *Police: Pakistan militants target women on bus, go after survivors at hospital.* Retrieved from http://www.cnn.com/2013/06/15/world/asia/pakistan-bomb/

National Association of Social Workers. (2017). Retrieved from www.socialworkers.org

Nicolai, S., Hine, S., & Wales, J. (2015). *Education in Emergencies and protracted crisis: Toward a strengthened response.* Background paper for the Oslo Summit on Education for Development. London: Overseas development Institute.

Nordberg, J. (2014). *The underground girls of Kabul: In search of a hidden resistance in Afghanistan.* United States: Crown Publishers.

Palumbo, S. (2012). *Meet the Graduates of the Oprah Winfrey Leadership Academy for Girls.* Published by O, The Oprah Winfrey Magazine.

Peters M. (2014). *"Western education is sinful": Boko Haram and the abduction of Chibok schoolgirls.* Policy Futures in Education, 12 (2)

Polaris. (2017). Retrieved from polarisproject.org

Popalzai, M., (May 2012). *Official: 160 girls poisoned at Afghan school.* Retrieved from
http://www.cnn.com/2012/05/29/world/asia/afghani
stan-girls-poisoned/

Save the Children, (2013). *The Right to Learn: Community Partnership in Improving Learning.* Retrieved from
http://www.savethechildren.org/atf/cf/
percent7B9def2ebe-10ae-432c-9bd0-df91d2eba74a
percent7D/THE_RIGHT_TO_LEARN.PDF

Save the Children (2016). *Every last girl: Free to live, free to learn, free from harm.* Retrieved from
http://www.savethechildren.org/atf/cf/
percent7B9def2ebe-10ae-432c-9bd0-df91d2eba74a
percent7D/EVERY percent20LAST percent20GIRL
percent20REPORT percent20FINAL.PDF

Schultz, P. (2002). *Why governments should invest more to educate girls.* World Development 30, No. 2: 207-225.

Shapiro J. (2015). *Michelle Obama tells global educators to Let Girls Learn.* Forbes Magazine.

Sperling, G. B., & Winthrop, R. (2016). *What works in girls' education: evidence for the world's best investment.* Washington, D.C.: Brookings Institution Press.

The Talko (2016). *10 Worst countries to be born a woman.* Retrieved from https://www.youtube.com/watch?v=sQdMN9MuIEE

*Times of India (*2011). *Of 11m abandoned children 20 percent are girls.*

United Nations. (2017). Retrieved from www.un.org

United Nations of Drug and Crime. (2017). Retrieved from www.unodc.org

United Nations Educational, Scientific and Cultural Organization. (2013). *Girls' education - the facts. Education for all Global Monitoring report.* Retrieved from http://en.unesco.org/gem-report/sites/gem-report/files/girls-factsheet-en.pdf

United Nations Educational, Scientific and Cultural Organization. (2014). *Teaching and Learning: Achieving Quality for All - EFA Global Monitoring Report 2013/4.* Paris: UNESCO.

United Nations Educational, Scientific and Cultural Organization. (2015). *Education for All 2000-2015: Achievements and Challenges - Education for all global monitoring report 2015.* Paris: UNESCO.

United Nations Population Fund. (2014). *Adding it Up: The Costs and Benefits of Investing in Sexual and Reproductive Health 2014.*
Retrieved from
http://www.unfpa.org/sites/default/files/pub-pdf/Adding percent20It percent20Up-Final-11.18.14.pdf

United Nations High Commissioner for Refugees. (2014). *World at War: Global Trends in Forced Displacement in 2014.* Geneva: UNHCR.

United Nations International Children's Emergency Fund. (2010). *Statement by UNICEF Executive Director Ann M. Veneman on International Women's Day: A time to focus on adolescent girls.* Retrieved from http://www.un.org/en/events/womensday/2010/documents/UNICEF_Ex_Dir_message.pdf

United Nations. (2017). Retrieved from www.un.org

U.S. Agency for International Development. (2016). *Promoting gender equality and access to education.* Retrieved from https://www.usaid.gov/what-we-do/gender-equality-and-womens-empowerment/addressing-gender-programming/promoting-gender

U.S. Agency for International Development. (2016). *Fact sheet: Let Girls Learn.* Retrieved from https://obamawhitehouse.archives.gov/sites/default/files/image/files/let_girls_learn_fact_sheet_03032015.pdf

Unterhalter E. & North A. (2011). *Girls' Schooling, Gender Equity and the Global Education and Development Agenda: Conceptual disconnections, political struggles and the difficulties of practice.* Feminist Formations. Volume 23, Issue 3, Fall 2011 pp. 1-22

Weir, S. (1999). *The effects of education on farmer productivity in rural Ethiopia.* Working Paper 99-7. Oxford: Centre for the Study of the African Economies.

Winthrop, R. & McGivney, E. (2014, September 23). *The top 10 list you don't want to be on: Dangerous places for girls' education.* Retrieved from https://www.brookings.edu/blog/education-plus-development/2014/09/23/the-top-10-list-you-dont-want-to-be-on-dangerous-places-for-girls-education/

World Health Organization. (2016). *Fact sheet: Maternal mortality.* Retrieved from http://www.who.int/mediacentre/factsheets/fs348/en

World Health Organization. (2016). *Fact sheet: Adolescent pregnancy.*

World Health Organization. (2016). *Fact Sheet: Children reducing mortality.*

Yousafzai, M. (2013). *I am Malala: The girls who stood up for education and was shot by the Taliban.* Brown and Company.

www.ingramcontent.com/pod-product-compliance
Lightning Source LLC
Chambersburg PA
CBHW062142280526
45788CB00001B/273